IMAGINE YOUR LIFE WITHOUT FEAR

MAX LUCADO

THOMAS NELSON
Since 1798

NASHVILLE   DALLAS   MEXICO CITY   RIO DE JANEIRO   BEIJING

Published in Nashville, Tennessee, by Thomas Nelson. Thomas Nelson is a
trademark of Thomas Nelson, Inc.

Thomas Nelson, Inc., titles may be purchased in bulk for educational,
business, fund-raising, or sales promotional use. For information, please
e-mail SpecialMarkets@ThomasNelson.com.

All material is adapted from *Fearless: Imagine Your Life Without Fear* and
The 3:16 Promise.

ISBN: 978-0-8499-2020-2

Printed in the United States of America

09 10 11 12 13 OPM 5 4 3 2

DEAR FRIEND,

Fear seems to be in the driver's seat these days. We are troubled and anxious. Finances are tumbling, rockets are launching, and seemingly solid institutions are teetering. It's tough to know where to turn, isn't it?

That's why I wanted you to have this message. There is an antidote to our fears—trust. If we trust God more, we can fear less. What a comforting promise.

Jesus didn't want us to live fearfully. He often reminded us, "Fear not." Looking at Jesus' statements about fear points us toward steadiness in the face of fearful circumstances.

The message in this little booklet is taken from my book *Fearless: Imagine Your Life Without Fear*. I hope a word or two from these pages will lift your spirits or help you encourage a friend. God doesn't want us to live in fear. Let's keep our gaze on Christ. Trust him, and fear less.

—MAX LUCADO

Contents

CHAPTER 1

Fear Knocks

Take courage. I am here!

—MATTHEW 14:27 NLT

You would have liked my brother. Everyone did. Dee made friends the way bakers make bread: daily, easily, warmly. Handshake—big and eager; laughter—contagious and volcanic. He permitted no stranger to remain one for long. I, the shy younger brother, relied on him to make introductions for us both. When a family moved onto the street or a newcomer walked onto the playground, Dee was the ambassador.

But in his midteen years, he made one acquaintance he should have avoided—a bootlegger who would sell beer to underage drinkers. Alcohol made a play for us both, but although it entwined me, it enchained him. Over the next four decades my brother drank away health, relationships, jobs, money, and all but the last two years of his life.

Who can say why resolve sometimes wins and sometimes loses, but at the age of fifty-four my brother discovered an aquifer of willpower, drilled deep, and enjoyed a season of sobriety. He emptied his bottles, stabilized his marriage, reached out to his children, and exchanged the liquor store for the local AA. But the hard living had taken its toll. Three decades of three-packs-a-day smoking had turned his big heart into ground meat.

On a January night during the week I began writing this book, he told Donna, his wife, that he couldn't breathe well. He already had a doctor's appointment for a related concern, so he decided to try to sleep. Little success. He awoke at 4:00 a.m. with chest pains severe enough to warrant a call to the emergency room. The rescue team loaded Dee on the gurney and told Donna to meet them at the hospital. My brother waved weakly and smiled bravely and told Donna not to worry, but by the time she and one of Dee's sons reached the hospital, he was gone.

The attending physician told them the news and invited them to step into the room where Dee's body lay. Holding each other, they walked through the doors and saw his final message. His hand was resting on the top of his thigh with the two center fingers folded in and the thumb extended, the universal sign-language symbol for "I love you."

I've tried to envision the final moments of my brother's earthly life: racing down a Texas highway in an ambulance through an inky night, paramedics buzzing around him, his heart weakening within him. Struggling for each breath, at some point he realized only a few remained. But rather than panic, he quarried some courage.

Perhaps you could use some. An ambulance isn't the only ride that demands valor. You may not be down to your final heartbeat, but you may be down to your last paycheck, solution, or thimble of faith. Each sunrise seems to bring fresh reasons for fear.

They're talking layoffs at work, slowdowns in the economy, flare-ups in the Middle East, turnovers at headquarters, downturns in the housing market, upswings in global warming, breakouts of al Qaeda cells. Some demented dictator is collecting nuclear warheads the way others collect fine wines. A strain of Asian flu is boarding flights out of China. The plague of our day, terrorism, begins with the word *terror*. News programs disgorge enough hand-wringing information to warrant an advisory. "Caution: this news report is best viewed in the confines of an underground vault in Iceland."

We fear being sued, finishing last, going broke; we fear the mole on the back, the new kid on the block, the sound of the clock as it ticks us closer to the grave. We sophisticate investment plans, create elaborate security systems, and legislate stronger military, yet we depend on mood-altering drugs more than any other generation in history. Moreover, "ordinary children today are more fearful than psychiatric patients were in the 1950s."[1]

Fear, it seems, has taken a hundred-year lease on the building next-door and set up shop. Oversize and rude, fear is unwilling to share the heart with happiness. Happiness complies. Do you ever see the two together? Can one be happy and afraid at the same time? Clear thinking and afraid? Confident and afraid? Merciful and afraid? No. Fear is the big bully in the high school hallway: brash, loud, and unproductive. For all the noise fear makes and room it takes, fear does little good.

Fear never wrote a symphony or poem, negotiated a peace treaty, or cured a disease. Fear never pulled a family out of poverty or a country out of bigotry. Fear never saved a marriage or a business. Courage did that. Faith did that. People who refused to consult or cower to their timidities did that. But fear itself? Fear herds us into a prison and slams the doors.

Wouldn't it be great to walk out?

Imagine your life wholly untouched by angst. What if faith, not fear, was your default reaction to threats? If you could hover a fear magnet over your heart and extract every last shaving of dread, insecurity, and doubt, what would remain? Envision a day, just one day, absent the dread of failure, rejection, and calamity.

CHAPTER 2

Why Are We Afraid?

Why are you fearful, O you of little faith?

—MATTHEW 8:26

Can you imagine a life with no fear? This is the possibility behind Jesus' question.

"Why are you afraid?" he asks (Matt. 8:26 NCV).

At first blush we wonder if Jesus is serious. He may be kidding. Teasing. Pulling a quick one. Kind of like one swimmer asking another, "Why are you wet?" But Jesus doesn't smile. He's dead earnest. So are the men to whom he asks the question. A storm has turned their Galilean dinner cruise into a white-knuckled plunge.

Here is how one of them remembered the trip: "Jesus got into a boat, and his followers went with him. A great storm arose on the lake so that waves covered the boat" (Matt. 8:23–24 NCV).

These are Matthew's words. He remembered well the pouncing tempest and bouncing boat and was careful in his terminology. Not just any noun would do. He pulled his Greek thesaurus off the shelf and hunted for a descriptor that exploded like the waves across the bow. He bypassed common terms for spring shower, squall, cloudburst, or downpour. They didn't capture what he felt and saw that night: a rumbling earth and quivering shoreline. He recalled more than winds and whitecaps. His finger followed the column of synonyms down, down until he landed on a word that worked. "Ah, there it is." *Seismos*—a quake, a trembling eruption of sea and sky. "A great *seismos* arose on the lake."

The term still occupies a spot in our vernacular. A *seis*mologist studies earthquakes, a *seis*mograph measures them, and Matthew, along with a crew of recent recruits, felt a seismos that shook them to the core. He used the word on only two other occasions: once at Jesus' death when Calvary shook (Matt. 27:51–54) and again at Jesus' resurrection when the graveyard tremored (28:2). Apparently, the stilled storm shares equal billing in the trilogy of Jesus' great shakeups: defeating sin on the cross, death at the tomb, and here silencing fear on the sea.

Sudden fear. We know the fear was sudden because the storm was. An older translation reads, "*Suddenly* a great tempest arose on the sea."

Not all storms come suddenly. Prairie farmers can see the formation of thunderclouds hours before the rain falls. This storm, however, springs like a lion out of the grass. One minute the disciples are shuffling cards for a midjourney game of hearts; the next they are gulping Galilean sea spray.

Peter and John, seasoned sailors, struggle to keep down the sail. Matthew, confirmed landlubber, struggles to keep down his breakfast. The storm is not what the tax collector bargained for. Do you sense his surprise in the way he links his two sentences? "Jesus got into a boat, and his followers went with him. A great storm arose on the lake" (8:23–24 NCV).

Wouldn't you hope for a more chipper second sentence, a happier consequence of obedience? "Jesus got into a boat. His followers went with him, and suddenly a great rainbow arched in the sky, a flock of doves hovered in happy formation, a sea of glass mirrored their mast." Don't Christ-followers enjoy a calendar full of Caribbean cruises?

No. This story sends the not-so-subtle and not-too-popular reminder: getting on board with Christ can mean getting soaked with Christ. Disciples can expect rough seas and stout winds. "In the world you will [not 'might,' 'may,' or 'could'] have tribulation" (John 16:33, brackets mine).

Christ-followers contract malaria, bury children, and battle addictions, and, as a result, face fears. It's not the absence of storms that sets us apart. It's whom we discover in the storm: an unstirred Christ.

"Jesus was sleeping" (v. 24 NCV).

Now there's a scene. The disciples scream; Jesus dreams. Thunder roars; Jesus snores. He doesn't doze, catnap, or rest. He slumbers. Could you sleep at a time like this? Could you snooze during a roller coaster loop-the-loop? In a wind tunnel? At a kettledrum concert? Jesus sleeps through all three at once!

Mark's Gospel adds two curious details:

"[Jesus] was in the stern, asleep on a pillow" (Mark 4:38). In the stern, on a pillow. Why the first? From whence came the second?

First-century fishermen used large, heavy seine nets for their work. They stored the nets in a nook that was built into the stern for this purpose. Sleeping *upon* the stern deck was impractical. It provided no space or protection. The small compartment beneath the stern, however, provided both. It was the most enclosed and only protected part of the boat. So Christ, a bit dozy from the day's activities, crawled beneath the deck to get some sleep.

He rested his head, not on a fluffy feather pillow, but on a leather sandbag. A ballast bag. Mediterranean fishermen still use them. They weigh about a hundred pounds and are used to ballast, or stabilize, the boat.[2] Did Jesus take the pillow to the stern so he could sleep, or sleep so soundly that someone rustled him up the pillow? We don't know. But this much we do know. This was a premeditated slumber. He didn't accidentally nod off. In full knowledge of the coming storm, Jesus decided it was siesta time, so he crawled into the corner, put his head on the pillow, and drifted into dreamland.

His snooze troubles the disciples. Matthew and Mark record their responses as three staccato Greek pronouncements and one question.

The pronouncements: "Lord! Save! Dying!" (Matt. 8:25).

The question: "Teacher, do You not care that we are perishing?" (Mark 4:38).

They do not ask about Jesus' strength: "Can you still the storm?" His knowledge: "Are you aware of the storm?" Or his know-how: "Do you have any experience with storms?" But rather, they raise doubts about Jesus' character: "Do you not care . . ."

Fear does this.

CHAPTER 3

Does
God Care?

Lord, save us! We are perishing!

—MATTHEW 8:25

Fear corrodes our confidence in God's goodness. We begin to wonder if love lives in heaven. If God can sleep in our storms, if his eyes stay shut when our eyes grow wide, if he permits storms after we get on his boat, does he care? Fear unleashes a swarm of doubts, anger-stirring doubts.

And it turns us into control freaks. "Do something about the storm!" is the implicit demand of the question. "Fix it or ... or ... or else!" Fear, at its center, is a perceived loss of control. When life spins wildly, we grab for a component of life we can manage: our diet, the tidiness of a house, the armrest of a plane, or, in many cases, people. The more insecure we feel, the meaner we become. We growl and bare our fangs. Why? Because we are bad? In part. But also because we feel cornered.

Martin Niemöller documents an extreme example of this. He was a German pastor who took a heroic stand against Adolf Hitler. When he first met the dictator in 1933, Niemöller stood at the back of the room and listened. Later, when his wife asked him what he'd learned, he said, "I discovered that Herr Hitler is a terribly frightened man."[3] Fear releases the tyrant within.

It also deadens our recall. The disciples had reason to trust Jesus. By now they'd seen him "healing all kinds of sickness and all kinds of disease among the people" (Matt.

4:23). They had witnessed him heal a leper with a touch and a servant with a command (Matt. 8:3, 13). Peter saw his sick mother-in-law recover (Matt. 8:14–15), and they all saw demons scatter like bats out of a cave. "He cast out the spirits with a word, and healed all who were sick" (Matt. 8:16).

Shouldn't someone mention Jesus' track record or review his résumé? Do they remember the accomplishments of Christ? They may not. Fear creates a form of spiritual amnesia. It dulls our miracle memory. It makes us forget what Jesus has done and how good God is.

And fear feels dreadful. It sucks the life out of the soul, curls us into an embryonic state, and drains us dry of contentment. We become abandoned barns, rickety and tilting from the winds, a place where humanity used to eat, thrive, and find warmth. No longer. When fear shapes our lives, safety becomes our god. When safety becomes our god, we worship the risk-free life. Can the safety lover do anything great? Can the risk-averse accomplish noble deeds? For God? For others? No. The fear-filled cannot love deeply. Love is risky. They cannot give to the poor. Benevolence has no guarantee of return. The fear-filled cannot dream wildly. What if their dreams sputter and fall from the sky? The worship of safety emasculates greatness. No wonder Jesus wages such a war against fear.

His most common command emerges from the "fear not" genre. The Gospels list some 125 Christ-issued imperatives. Of these, 21 urge us to "not be afraid" or "not fear" or "have courage" or "take heart" or "be of good cheer." The second most common command, to love God and neighbor, appears on only eight occasions. If quantity is any indicator, Jesus takes our fears seriously. The one statement he made more than any other was this: don't be afraid.

Siblings sometimes chuckle at or complain about the most common command of their parents. They remember how Mom was always saying, "Be home on time," or, "Did you clean your room?" Dad had his favorite directives too. "Keep your chin up." "Work hard." I wonder if the disciples ever reflected on the most-often-repeated phrases of Christ. If so, they would have noted, "He was always calling us to courage."

> So don't be afraid. You are worth
> much more than many sparrows.
> (Matt. 10:31 NCV)

> I tell you not to worry about
> everyday life—whether you have
> enough. (Matt. 6:25 NLT)

> Take courage. I am here! (Matt.
> 14:27 NLT)

> Do not fear those who kill the

body but cannot kill the soul.
(Matt. 10:28)

Don't let your hearts be troubled.
Trust in God, and trust also in
me. . . . I will come and get you, so
that you will always be with me
where I am. (John 14:1, 3 NLT)

Don't be troubled or afraid. (John
14:27 NLT)

You will hear of wars and rumors
of wars, but see to it that you are
not alarmed. (Matt. 24:6 NIV)

Jesus came and touched them and
said, "Arise, and do not be afraid."
(Matt. 17:7)

Jesus doesn't want you to live in a state
of fear. Nor do you. You've never made
statements like these:

My phobias put such a spring in my
step.
I'd be a rotten parent were it not for
my hypochondria.
Thank God for my pessimism. I've
been such a better person since
I lost hope.
My doctor says if I don't begin
fretting, I will lose my health.

We've learned the high cost of fear.

Jesus' question is a good one. He lifts his head from the pillow, steps out from the stern into the storm, and asks, "Why are you fearful, O you of little faith?" (Matt. 8:26).

To be clear, fear serves a healthy function. It is the canary in the coal mine, warning of potential danger. A dose of fright can keep a child from running across a busy road or an adult from smoking a pack of cigarettes. Fear is the appropriate reaction to a burning building or growling dog. Fear itself is not a sin. But it can lead to sin.

If we medicate fear with angry outbursts, drinking binges, sullen withdrawals, self-starvation, or viselike control, we exclude God from the solution and exacerbate the problem. We subject ourselves to a position of fear, allowing anxiety to dominate and define our lives. Joy-sapping worries. Day-numbing dread. Repeated bouts of insecurity that petrify and paralyze us. Hysteria is not from God. "For God has not given us a *spirit* of fear" (2 Tim. 1:7).

Fear will always knock on your door. Just don't invite it in for dinner, and for heaven's sake don't offer it a bed for the night. Let's embolden our hearts with a select number of Jesus' "do not fear" statements. Fear may fill our world, but it doesn't have to fill our hearts. The promise of Christ and the contention of this book are simple: we can fear less tomorrow than we do today.

When I was six years old, my dad let me stay up late with the rest of the family and watch the movie *The Wolf Man*. Boy, did he regret that decision. The film left me convinced that the Wolf Man spent each night prowling our den, awaiting his preferred meal of first grade, redheaded, freckle-salted boy. My fear proved problematic. To reach the kitchen from my bedroom, I had to pass perilously close to his claws and fangs, something I was loath to do. More than once I retreated to my father's bedroom and awoke him. Like Jesus in the boat, Dad was sound asleep in the storm. *How can a person sleep at a time like this?*

Opening a sleepy eye, he would ask, "Now, why are you afraid?" And I would remind him of the monster. "Oh yes, the Wolf Man," he'd grumble. He would then climb out of bed, arm himself with superhuman courage, escort me through the valley of the shadow of death, and pour me a glass of milk. I would look at him with awe and wonder, *What kind of man is this?*

God views our seismos storms the way my father viewed my wolf man angst. "Jesus got up and gave a command to the wind and the waves, and it became completely calm" (Matt. 8:26 NCV).

He handles the great quaking with a great calming. The sea becomes as still as a frozen lake, and the disciples are left wondering, "What kind of man is this? Even the winds and the waves obey him!" (v. 27 NCV).

What kind of man, indeed. Turning typhoon time into nap time. Silencing waves with one word. And equipping a dying man with sufficient courage to send a final love message to his family. Way to go, Dee. You faced your share of seismos moments in life, but in the end you didn't go under.

Here's a prayer that we won't either.

CHAPTER 4

The Ultimate Fear

Don't let your hearts be troubled.
Trust in God, and trust also in me.

—JOHN 14:1 NLT

Aristotle called death the thing to be feared most because "it appears to be the end of everything."[4] Jean-Paul Sartre asserted that death "removes all meaning from life."[5] Robert Green Ingersoll, one of America's most outspoken agnostics, could offer no words of hope at his brother's funeral. He said, "Life is a narrow vale between the cold and barren peaks of two eternities. We strive in vain to look beyond the heights."[6] The pessimism of French philosopher François Rabelais was equally arctic. He made this sentence his final one: "I am going to the great Perhaps."[7]

Such sad, depressing language! If death is nothing more than "the end of everything," "barren peaks," and "the great Perhaps," what is the possibility of dying bravely? But what if the philosophers missed it? Suppose death is different than they thought, less a curse and more a passageway, not a crisis to be avoided but a corner to be turned?

This is the promise of Christ: "Don't let your hearts be troubled. Trust in God, and trust also in me. There is more than enough room in my Father's home. If this were not so, would I have told you that I am going to prepare a place for you? When everything is ready, I will come and get you, so that you will always be with me where I am" (John 14:1–3 NLT). Have you claimed his promise?

If not, maybe it's because it sounds too good to be true.

"Free flight: Rio de Janeiro to Miami, Florida."

I wasn't the only person to hear about the offer but one of the few to phone and request details. The courier service offered an airline ticket to anyone willing to carry a bag of mail to the States. The deal was tantalizingly simple:

Meet the company representative at the airport, where you'll be given a duffel bag of documents and one ticket. Check the bag when you check in for the flight. Retrieve the bag in Miami before you make your connection. Give it to the uniformed courier representative, who'll await you beyond customs.

No company makes such offers anymore. But this was 1985—years before intense airport security. My dad was dying of ALS, airline tickets expensive, and my checking account as thin as a Paris supermodel. Free ticket? The offer sounded too good to be true.

So I walked away from it.

Many do the same with an offer found in John 3:16:

"For God so loved the world that he gave his one and only Son, that whoever believes in him shall not perish but have eternal life" (NIV).

Millions read the verse. Only a handful trust it. Wary of a catch perhaps? Not needy enough maybe? Cautioned by guarded friends?

I was. Other Rio residents saw the same offer. Some read it and smelled a rat.

"Don't risk it," one warned me. "Better to buy your own ticket."

But I couldn't afford one. Each call to Mom brought worse news.

"He's back in the hospital."

"Unable to breathe without oxygen."

"The doctor says it's time to call hospice."

So I revisited the flyer. Desperation heightened my interest.

Doesn't it always?

When he asks for a divorce or she says, "It's over." When the coroner calls, the kids rebel, or the finances collapse. When desperation typhoons into your world, God's offer of a free flight home demands a second look. John 3:16 morphs from a nice verse to a life vest.

Some of you are wearing it. You can recount the day you put it on. For you, the passage comforts like your favorite blanket:

God so loved . . .

believes in him . . .

shall not perish . . .

eternal life.

These words have kept you company through multiple windswept winters. I pray they warm you through the ones that remain.

Others of you are still studying the flyer. Still pondering the possibility, wrestling with the promise. One day wondering what kind of fool offer this is, the next wondering what kind of fool would turn it down.

I urge you not to. Don't walk away from this one. Who else can get you home? Who else has turned his grave into a changing closet and offered to do the same with yours? Take Jesus' offer. Get on board. You don't want to miss this chance to see your Father.

I didn't. I called the company and signed up. Denalyn drove me to the airport. I found the courier employee, accepted the passage, checked the bag, and took my seat on the plane, smiling like I'd just found a forgotten gift under the Christmas tree.

Do likewise. You don't need to go to the airport, but you do need to make a move. You need to give God your answer: "Christ will live in you as you open the door and invite him in" (Eph. 3:17 MSG). Say yes to him. Your prayer needs no eloquence, just honesty.

Father, I believe you love this world. You gave your one and only Son so I can live forever with you. Apart from you, I die. With you, I live. I choose life. I choose you.

If you aren't sure you've told him, you haven't. We can't get on board and not know it. Nor can we get on board and hide it. No stowaways permitted. Christ-followers go public with their belief. We turn from bad behavior to good (repentance). We stop following our passions and salute our new captain (confession). We publicly demonstrate our devotion (baptism).[8]

We don't keep our choice a secret. Why would we? We're on our way home for Christ's sake.

Thanks to the courier folks, I was present at my father's death.

Thanks to God, he'll be present at yours.

He cares too much not to be. Believe in him
and you
> will ...
>> not ...
>>> perish.
You will have life, eternal life, forever.

CHAPTER 5

Fear Not: God's Promises

I will be with you always.

—MATTHEW 28:20 NIV

WHEN WE FEAR WE DON'T MATTER

"So don't be afraid. You are worth much more than many sparrows." (Matt. 10:31 NCV)

"For we are God's masterpiece. He has created us anew in Christ Jesus, so we can do the good things he planned for us long ago." (Eph. 2:10 NLT)

WHEN WE FEAR WE'VE DISAPPOINTED GOD

"Take courage, son; your sins are forgiven." (Matt. 9:2 NASB)

"If we confess our sins, He is faithful and just to forgive us our sins and to cleanse us from all unrighteousness." (1 John 1:9 NKJV)

WHEN FEAR BECOMES WORRY

"I tell you not to worry about everyday life—whether you have enough. Look at the birds. They don't plant or harvest or store food in barns, for your heavenly Father feeds them. And aren't you far more valuable to him than they are? Can all your worries add a single moment to your life?" (Matt. 6:25–27 NLT)

"Your heavenly Father already knows all

your needs. Seek the Kingdom of God above all else, and live righteously, and he will give you everything you need." (Matt. 6:32–33 NLT)

WHEN WE FEAR WE'RE NOT PROTECTING OUR KIDS

"Don't be afraid. Just believe, and your daughter will be well." (Luke 8:50 NCV)

"Pour out your heart like water before the face of the Lord. Lift your hands toward Him for the life of your young children." (Lam. 2:19 NKJV)

WHEN WE FEAR OVERWHELMING CHALLENGES

"Don't be afraid," he said. "Take courage. I am here!" (Matt. 14:27 NLT)

"Nothing can ever separate us from God's love. Neither death nor life, neither angels nor demons, neither our fears for today nor our worries about tomorrow—not even the powers of hell can separate us from God's love." (Rom. 8:38 NLT)

WHEN WE FEAR
WORST-CASE SCENARIOS

"God's looking after me, keeping me safe in the kingdom of heaven. All praise to him, praise forever!" (2 Tim. 4:18 MSG)

"Stay awake and pray for strength." (Matt. 26:41 NCV)

WHEN WE FEAR VIOLENCE

"Do not fear those who kill the body but cannot kill the soul." (Matt. 10:28)

"Can anything separate us from the love Christ has for us? Can troubles or problems or sufferings or hunger or nakedness or danger or violent death? . . . Nothing above us, nothing below us, nor anything else in the whole world will ever be able to separate us from the love of God that is in Christ Jesus our Lord." (Rom. 8:35, 39 NCV)

WHEN WE FEAR FINANCIAL ADVERSITY

"Do not fear, little flock, for it is your Father's good pleasure to give you the kingdom." (Luke 12:32)

"Do not worry about your life. . . . Do not seek what you should eat or what you should drink, nor have an anxious mind." (Luke 12: 22, 29)

WHEN WE FEAR LIFE'S
FINAL MOMENTS

"Don't let your hearts be troubled. Trust in God, and trust also in me. There is more than enough room in my Father's home. If this were not so, would I have told you that I am going to prepare a place for you? When everything is ready, I will come and get you, so that you will always be with me where I am." (John 14:1–3 NLT)

"Christ was raised as the first of the harvest; then all who belong to Christ will be raised when he comes back." (1 Cor. 15:23 NLT)

WHEN WE FEAR WHAT'S NEXT

"When the Father sends the Advocate as my representative—that is, the Holy Spirit—he will teach you everything and will remind you of everything I have told you. I am leaving you with a gift—peace of mind and heart. And the peace I give is a gift the world cannot give. So don't be troubled or afraid." (John 14:26–27 NLT)

"Surely goodness and mercy shall follow me all the days of my life." (Ps. 23:6)

WHEN WE FEAR THAT
GOD IS NOT REAL

"Look at my hands. Look at my feet. You can see that it's really me. Touch me and make sure that I am not a ghost, because ghosts don't have bodies, as you see that I do." As he spoke, he showed them his hands and his feet." (Luke 24:39–40 NLT)

"Lord, I believe; help my unbelief!" (Mark 9:24)

WHEN WE FEAR
GLOBAL CALAMITY

"You will hear of wars and rumors of wars, but see to it that you are not alarmed." (Matthew 24:6 NIV)

"Though a host encamp against me, my heart shall not fear; though war arise against me, yet I will be confident." (Ps. 27:3 RSV)

WHEN WE FEAR WE DON'T
REALLY KNOW GOD

"He was transfigured before them. His face shone like the sun, and His clothes became as white as the light. . . . They fell on their faces and were greatly afraid. But Jesus came and touched them and said, 'Arise, and do not be afraid.'" (Matt. 17:2, 6–7)

"The fear of the Lord leads to life, and he who has it will abide in satisfaction; He will not be visited with evil." (Prov. 19:23)

Notes

1. *The Report Newsmagazine*, January 22, 2001,
   Candis McLean. http://findarticles.com/
   plarticles/m_hb3543/is_2001/01/
   ai_n8359052?tag=content;col1.
2. Shelley Wachsmann, *The Sea of Galilee Boat:
   An Extraordinary 2000 Year Old Discovery*
   (New York: Plenum Press, 1995), 326--28.
3. Walter Brueggemann, "The Liturgy of
   Abundance, the Myth of Scarcity," *Christian
   Century*, March 24–31, 1999, http://www.reli-
   gion-online.org/showarticle.asp?title=533.
4. Donald G. Bloesch, *The Last Things:
   Resurrection, Judgment, Glory* (Downers Grove,
   IL: InterVarsity Press, 2004), 125.
5. Ibid.
6. John Blanchard, *Whatever Happened to Hell?*
   (Wheaton, IL: Crossway Books, 1995), 63.
7. Ibid, 62.
8. Acts 26:20; Rom. 10:9; Acts 2:38.

Share the
Fearless Message!

Utilize the *Fearless* booklet and book to:

➤ Share with your small group or congregants for a church-wide study

➤ Hand out to your community as an outreach tool at events, service outings, etc.

➤ Provide as encouragement for people in economic, physical, or spiritual need

Fearless
978-0-8499-2139-1

Imagine Your Life Without Fear
978-0-8499-2020-2

For information about bulk purchase of these *Fearless* products, contact your local retailer.

THOMAS NELSON
Since 1798

www.maxlucado.com